Live Streaming is Smart Marketing

Presented by the StreamGeeks

By Paul William Richards

ISBN: 9781704947372

DEDICATION

To my daughter Annabel.

CONTENTS

Chapter 1: Update!

Since the original publication of this book in February of 2018 a lot has changed. Our team has traveled around the world from TwitchCon, to IBC, NAB, and many more streaming media focused events in search of like minded individuals. Our team has even hosted our own StreamGeeks Summit in New York City, to deliver a full day of live streaming education to the world. Over the past few years live streaming has been growing at an unprecedented rate with huge social and shopping networks such as LinkedIn and Amazon jumping on board. The live streaming landscape is changing quickly and it's never been more exciting to be part of this ever evolving industry.

Therefore, this book is now in edition #2. New chapters have been added outlining best practices for Amazon, LinkedIn and the IRL (In Real Life) streaming phenomenon. Each chapter adds to our experience tweaking the technology and presentation strategies that we have found most effective for each unique live video platform. I hope you enjoy this new update and do not hesitate to join our active Facebook User Group at https://facebook.com/groups/streamgeeks.

This book is about the thought-process that lead to the start of StreamGeeks. A story that is equal parts marketing, video production, and inspiration. If you are interested in more in-depth tutorials or subject matter focused content consider checking out one of my other books noted below.

1. Helping Your Church Live Stream

2. The Unofficial Guide to Open Broadcaster Software

3. The Accelerated Broadcast Club Curriculum

Chapter 2: How We Got Here

GEEK
MARKETING TIP

Don't forget to upload your video content natively to each social media platform. Video always performs better when it's native to the platform

After about a year of live streaming, making every mistake in the book, I realized that creating live video was starting to become easy for me. The rubber was really starting to hit the road for me creatively. Facebook live had just come out and instead of resisting the latest trending technology, I started simulcasting our show. Simulcasting became a new term in the industry, which described streaming media that was sent to multiple destinations at the same time. For the first time I was able to live stream our show to both YouTube and Facebook effectively doubling our audience. The seas were starting to open and our live show was on a roll.

So a couple times each week, I would live stream to the businesses social media accounts. I made a deal with our boss at the time that these live streams would only take up 10% of my work week. The promise to work half a day per week quickly spiraled into something much more. But this is where the story begins. I quickly realized that my job would become learning about something useful and sharing that knowledge with our audience. The more useful the knowledge I shared, the better it would perform. The SEO (Search Engine Optimization) landscape was at a time when it very much favored video content and most topics we covered had little competition. The more compelling our story and inbound marketing strategy was, the more leads we were able to create for our company.

At one point, I was making one video per day because there was so much content that needed to be cataloged and made into video. We decided to divide the week up into a "daily vlog schedule" which was something like: Mondays with Paul, Tech Support Tuesday, Back to Basics, Something New Thursday, and the regular Friday Show. I have to say that daily video creation did a lot for our YouTube channel. As long as we had a topic to talk about, we would sit down and record a presentation with prepared media.

VIDEO PRODUCTION HACK

Don't forget to have B-Roll ready during your live broadcasts. It's interesting for the viewer, but it also gives your talent a moment to prepare off camera.

We could have it uploaded to Facebook and/or YouTube as soon as we were finished recording. Since we recorded the whole video live, the real art was managing the video production software controls and talking about the given topic at the same time.

So here I am, sitting at the head of our company's conference room table, looking into a camera and a projector screen. The projection screen was just above the camera, so I was able to operate the video switcher and deliver my message to the camera at the same time. One video production hack I learned quickly was the power of B-Roll. I would play a pre-recorded video and read from a script that I had printed out in front of me. This was a way of making video creation almost too easy, because all I had to do was prepare some b-roll and read from a script. I would play an intro clip, introduce the topic on camera, roll the b-roll and read my notes. I must have produced 150 videos in this manner and it really jump started our digital footprint. To this day, I use b-roll video every chance I get.

That conference room and the pull down green screen we had installed are now ancient history. The videos we made generated well over 2 million views and who knows how many leads for our company. But even more importantly, something amazing came from the hustle. I was starting to understand how valuable video could be for our business. Today we live stream to YouTube, Facebook, Twitch, and LinkedIn.

When you start to see the true value of something, you don't want the process to be too easy. It's supposed to be hard work and I wanted to challenge myself to do better. To top it off, I was starting to get bogged down with the social media responsibilities. Real people from all around the world were messaging us at a rate that I couldn't handle by myself. It was becoming a full time job just responding to the YouTube comments and Facebook messages pouring in. This is of course a good problem to have □.

So out of this success came an even greater step forward when we hired Tess Protesto, our Social Media Manager. Tess eventually helped me start StreamGeeks and currently works as my amazing co-host. Tess was a West Chester University graduate, who already knew how to work with Facebook and manage social media. She has a bachelor's degree in communications and was happy to see our social media accounts with so much activity. Tess was also very interested in our live streaming show and

joined the show to host a small segment on our social media each week.

Together we built our first "real studio" in the nook of our office conference room. Her husband who works in the sign business was able to print out a blue brick vinyl sticker for the background.

We spent roughly $1,000 on the set which included shelving, bar stools and a cool white bar height service desk for us to stand behind. We actually still have a video tutorial course that we made throughout the process. This course is available on Udemy.com if you would like to learn more. So we made a plan and documented the studio build process.

We started our studio design ideas on Pinterest. Tess would "pin" design ideas on her "live show" board and we would go back and forth imagining what the set should look like. This real world experience helped us picture the possibilities of live streaming for business. We learned that positioning camera angles on a set should influence where you hang items like shelves. We also learned that less is more and the focus should be on our presentation. While handpicked items chosen to support your brand are nice, the focus should always be on your content.

At this time, I was still used to sitting in front of my green screen during the live broadcasts. So we continued to use a virtual set and we added a second camera for Tess in front of the new set we built. The virtual set was really professional looking and it actually fooled many of our viewers into thinking we had a city skyline view outside our production studio. I guess it did look as though we were somehow bringing in Tess for our "Social Media Update" from a remote location in downtown New York City. Let's not forget that this was the very first year that Facebook Live streaming was available in 2016. Most people on the platform had no idea what type of content would be available. Our video quality was so much better than the average cell phone streamer, I guess there was just magic in the air.

Looking back at all our broadcasts, I have to say that the quality still surprises me. We were able to bring in live callers from around the world and we took our show seriously. At this time many people said you only needed to live stream in 1280x720p resolution. I didn't listen and I always used Full HD 1080p quality. Looking back I'm so glad our archived video is in Full HD quality.

We would stick to a very professional agenda providing our guests a ten minute time slot to answer questions with a sixty second countdown timer for each question. I was trying very hard to respect the time of our viewers and keep us on tight schedule. I designed the visual agenda display based off of a popular ESPN show. We would prepare 8 custom PNG files for each show that would play with a "ding" every time we moved on to the next subject. I know our audience respected the television style feel we were going for. The quality of our production increased engagement and delivered to the content delivery networks (YouTube and Facebook) what they are looking for. Social signals triggered the platforms to share our content with larger and larger audiences each week. Today we know that by simply acknowledging live viewers by name and responding to comments is by far the best form of engagement.

Chapter 3: A Co-Host Joins the Team

Having a co-host is perhaps the best thing that happened to our live show and video production. Suddenly, I had someone to talk to and engage with in-studio throughout our presentation. While the show was almost always interview based in the beginning, having a second person in the studio made a huge difference in our production quality. It was easy to see that our live show viewership was growing significantly. Since I was still handling all of the video switching, Tess was able to focus on the chatroom and interject with questions from the audience. Tess's segment on Social Media would become a centerpiece of the show over time. Tess would highlight customer success stories and popular comments from Instagram or Facebook that promoted positive engagement with our viewers.

This was the real start of our online community. It was Tess's idea to make a bigger deal about what was going on with our Facebook and Instagram accounts. In turn, viewers became more active both during the show and after on social media. This was also the birth of our Facebook User groups which are still alive and well today. I will go into more detail about the value of Facebook Groups in a future chapter. I would encourage anyone interested in StreamGeeks to join our group and see the unique interactions going on.

Needless to say we were starting to move in the right direction. Slowly I was seeing the potential of creating television quality content from our companies conference room. We would take over the conference room all day on Fridays and storm out of the room like rock stars after a successful show. The viewership statistics were very encouraging. In just one hour, we would accumulate days' worth of face time with viewers around the world. I should mention that before we started our live segment we used to host weekly webinars. These webinars always had poor attendance and the production quality wasn't worth rewatching on-demand. We found that eliminating the barrier of entry that webinar registrations and downloads required made our viewership number 10X. Today we are getting fifty times as many viewers as our old webinar platform.

As the show progressed, we would start preparations earlier and play pump-up music before each broadcast. I really think that playing pump up music before your live broadcasts can increase the talent's on screen confidence. When you hit that "go live" button, Tess and I would take a deep breath and jump into our agenda. If our guest was interesting and our questions were engaging, viewers would stay for the entire hour long broadcast.

As time went on, we slowly moved away from the green screen and virtual set layout. Ultimately, I would join Tess in our blue brick set which was slowly accumulating new items such as the "On Air" light and a new behind the scenes camera. I realized that we could use multiple cameras in a way that could not be done in the virtual set. We started to add more and more cameras to our setup in order to capture the attention of our audience in different ways. We added an over the shoulder style camera for myself and a ceiling camera for overhead views. We even set up a close up camera with a wide angle lens for Tess to deliver her Social Media segments. We also installed a tally-light system which provided red lights on the top of each camera. These lights would sync up with our video production software to let us know which camera to look at.

Since I was still the solo producer of the show, I had two options. I could either control the entire broadcast looking up and down from a computer screen in front of me or I could have the software set to run on a playlist. A playlist can cycle through our show automatically. During some shows we would have the entire presentation planned out in a playlist. The playlist setup would determine how much time it would take in between camera transitions and other segments in a list automatically. I thought this was pretty high tech at the time. Today we have a human producer which is obviously the best choice when our teams resources allowed for it.

The video production was really starting to get better and our audience was starting to take notice. We would get offers from other companies to send us free gear just to have their products reviewed on our YouTube channel. We were booking out guests to join our show months in advance and we were always adding new live streaming techniques to the show. One cool addition to the show, was displaying live comments from YouTube and Facebook at the same time on the screen. We did this with a custom API we created. Today it's so much easier with the tools that are available in most production software.

Around this time, many of our audience members would give us detailed advice on how we could improve our show. Sometimes these critique comments would come across a little odd because we were so happy with the quality of our video production. In the midst of our live production, it almost sounded insulting when an audience member would say that we needed to add more lights or that the audio for our far end guest needed a compressor. Many of these early comments were ignored but I realized over time that our audience was giving us real-time advice we could use to improve our next live video production. In response, we started to extend the length of the pre-show and check in with our regular viewers. The process was like live streaming boot camp. We would often tweak some part of our show every week. The changes often came right down to the wire while the live countdown timer was ticking down to the show start. If you work well under pressure or deadlines, live streaming may fit your personality well as it did for me.

This was the very beginning of our crowdsourcing knowledge. We didn't know it yet, but this type of community engagement is the reward for putting yourself out there. The quality of our production today is a direct result of the advice given to us by our audience over the past three years. But before I get into the studio we have today, let me tell you a little bit about how we started StreamGeeks.

Chapter 4: Starting the StreamGeeks

Our live streams were starting to gain a lot of traction. Each week we were creating really great content for our business and our viewers. I always felt the desire to get more and more creative. I wanted to push the boundaries of what was possible in live streaming. One day we decided to fly a drone over our company's solar panels while we interviewed the manufacturer about the panel efficiency. While our audience was almost always entertained, some of our show ideas were a little "off brand" for our company. So we had a meeting with our team and decided we would create a new channel dedicated to the subject of live streaming. We would take just one day out of each week and focus on a more broadly defined live streaming channel. This channel would be able make connections and content with a further reach than our current brands (which were product focused). So we made a deal to keep our main brand "PTZOptics" and its channel completely brand focused. This opened the door for a whole new world of possibilities. Our show was really the basis for our research, development, and crowd-sourced critiquing. This channel would give us a platform to talk about anything we found interesting in the streaming world.

I can't remember every name we considered but "geek," "nerd," "tech," and "streaming" were all words we kept trying to jam together. We knew that our audience was geeky and we knew that we wanted to focus on the live streaming industry. Eventually someone mentioned "StreamGeeks" and we all said "YES!" So we bought the website domain and searched around for a Wordpress theme that we liked. It's amazing what a good name will do for a company.

In the beginning, it was supposed to be a simple podcast format show that we live streamed to YouTube and Facebook. A place where we could take a step back and review the past year or two of our own live streaming journey. We wanted to present content in a way that almost anyone could relate to. Our very first episode—which had absolutely no live viewers by the way—was called "Our Ah-Ha moments in live streaming". Tess and I sat down in-front of our blue brick studio and had the cameras set to cycle as we conversed about easy to digest live streaming topics.

We were quickly able to attract an audience interested in this type of content. Each week, Tess and I would think of a new idea that usually derived from some comment on Facebook or YouTube. We had a community just big enough to gather ideas about what people would want to see next.

I still remember getting our first 100 YouTube subscribers. Tess is great at being able to talk about almost any subject and ask thoughtful questions that provoke a larger discussion. Every time we mentioned our new Facebook User Group on the live show, we would have two or three more requests to join. Slowly everything was growing at a steady pace.

SOCIAL MEDIA TIP

Try adding a custom outro to each of your videos asking viewers to subscribe to your channel. Give them a compelling reason to keep coming back for more.

So StreamGeeks was started, but it wasn't quite launched. Over the next couple of months, we brought on a video production expert, named Michael Luttermoser, who would become our producer. In the beginning, Michael would watch our show and see how I was operating vMix. vMix is the video production software we use to transition between multiple cameras and display all of our graphics. Eventually, Michael was able to take over all the video production controls and allow Tess and I the freedom to simply be the on camera talent.

Knowing what it takes to operate the entire live streaming system and be on camera cut my teeth in the industry. In fact, some people said they loved seeing us operate the show on camera, even when we would make a mistake. But I knew, that in order to increase our video production quality overall, a dedicated producer was going to be key.

Things continued to progress. Business was good and our ambitions grew. We were a talented group of guerilla marketers with a budget. We had access to almost any audio visual equipment we could ever need. We could also advertise any of the content we felt was exceptionally powerful and all of this helped us grow our audience on Facebook and YouTube. It was a fun time and we continued to push the boundaries of what was possible.

In April of 2017, we hosted the world's first "Streaming Awards" dedicated to shows that are available exclusively on social media networks like YouTube or Facebook live. The show had a huge turnout with over 5,000 views in the first hour. The "2017 Streaming Awards Show" as we called it, was perhaps our most ambitious show to date. It was the first time we invited the public to our office. It was an exhilarating feeling to have a real live in-studio audience during the show. The show went off without a hitch and contestants from all around the world were celebrated for their work. We used a very fancy looking award ceremony Adobe After Effects template that took hours to render for each clip. Each video clip was accompanied by a professional voiceover and music. The production quality looked great and some of our in-studio audience even came on the show for interviews. One local school district was nominated for their daily school announcements show. It was a blast!

As we continued to grow it was obvious that we had started something that would outgrow our current office space. Tess and Michael were actually working in hallway cubicle spaces and the transition between a live broadcast and regular office desk work didn't fit into our creative workflow. So, we would take creativity walks around the business park. We would walk for hours sometimes talking about how the live show could be changed. We would talk about what the next topic could be and how the live viewers were responding to our content. These are still some of my fondest moments from our old office location.

Chapter 5: The New Studio

So long story short, we opened up a new office in downtown West Chester, Pennsylvania. The town is a perfect fit for our small marketing team. Each day I would skateboard through town and it was a thrill. West Chester is full of activity and other small businesses for the StreamGeeks to interact with. We joined the local Chamber of Commerce and hosted a ribbon cutting ceremony that we live streamed to Facebook.

At this point, I could see how the power of live streaming was still foreign to most other businesses in our community. We had roughly 80 people watching our ribbon cutting ceremony online. I made a joke about how we had more live viewers on Facebook than people actually attending the grand opening in person. Listening to the questions local business people had about live streaming and marketing was very eye opening. This was the start of StreamGeeks. The friction between our goals and real world businesses remains the source of our most interesting content.

I was able to convince our boss that the new office would be a showroom for what the live streaming industry could become in the future. We designed the office around the main broadcast studio and included other essential rooms such as post production and hair/makeup. We wanted to build the studio on a budget that almost any business could afford. But in all honesty, we kept spending more and more money on the studio. Our initial budget was $10,000 for all the furniture, networking equipment and other essentials. We were actually under budget initially but then we hired some painters to spruce up the place. They put up our signature red brick wallpaper and they also put us over budget. We continue to add equipment almost every week and the total studio budget is somewhat of a mystery.

If there is one thing I have learned about video production studios, it's that they are never finished. My wife, Lauren, played a significant role in designing the new office and our set. We discovered that less is more for set design. We presented potential studio designs to our audience before the move on our live show. We had multiple 3D Google Sketch-up designs that we would with our audience. During these shows I was really fishing for good advice from our viewers. These episodes performed extraordinarily well because it was an interesting topic for everyone involved. I spent hours looking at other live streaming studios to determine how everything could be setup. One show that has a great setup is the Twit Network with Leo Laporte. I saw a segment in one of his shows where he has a D-shaped standing height table with an LCD monitor at the end displaying his logo. This set along with countless others became the inspiration for our new studio.

Our set was also designed with a D-Shaped bar height table presentation area. The table has an LCD monitor mounted where the D-Shape meets the wall. This space allows two presenters to easily face the camera. We have ample space for product presentations and convenient camera angles for the production. I really like the standing height desks because it keeps the blood flowing during our broadcast. My wife suggested that we keep the rest of our studio open so that we could change the space

up from time to time. This was great advice because we regularly bring in different furniture and green screen materials when needed for specific shows. It's supposed to be a creative space, so maintaining openness has worked wonders for our setup. We are now able to bring all kinds of furniture in and out of our studio with ease.

Moving into a new

office takes time and building out a studio does as well. Somehow we were able to host our regular live shows without skipping a single episode. Since our show was all about live streaming, we made the move-in process part of the live show and we got a great response. Many of our viewers are in the midst of designing a live show or thinking about how they could implement at least some part of our plan in their own studios. We did not miss the chance to document the before and after process of building a live streaming studio, being the young marketing guerrillas that we are. Documenting your business process can become a great inspiration for your viewers. You can search our Facebook User Group and find others in the midst of building their own live streaming studios who drew inspiration from our move-in videos.

Chapter 6: Who is your Chief Streaming Officer?

I should start by saying that I absolutely love Australians and their uncanny knack for creating catchy slogans. I have to thank our Australian business partners for jokingly calling me the "Chief Streaming Officer" at a business dinner in Las Vegas. The business meeting was right after the National Association of Broadcasters show in 2016. We were discussing the massive business opportunities in the streaming industry and our joint success in the market. It was a very entertaining meeting filled with laughter and folly. After a few beers, one of our business partners said to me, "Well mate, I guess that makes you the Chief Streaming Officer."

The Chief Streaming Officer is a position that I believe every fortune 1000 company should have working at the top level of their organizations. When you look at the data on the value of video versus the cost of sales people the reason for fostering a dedicated live streaming team becomes quite obvious. Salesforce.com published a report noting that "a video with 7,500 views per day = 46 hyper efficient sales people working non-stop 8 hour days." The report shows how video can reach people faster and more effectively than traditional cold-calling sales personnel. Now take that thought and pair it with the limitless advertising Facebook and Google offer for roughly $.01/view.

These are powerful statistics that can question the way many businesses are run today. The market research firm Gartner published a report noting, "By 2020, customers will manage 85% of their interactions with the enterprise without interacting with a human." So, taking a step back and looking at the changes that are clearly sweeping the global economy, we can see that the value of video is increasing rapidly. At the same time, I could see that the cost to create high quality video content was actually coming down. It was the perfect storm!

So with this knowledge, I started to speak with local businesses and present on stage at conferences. I found that everyone acknowledges the value of video. This is one of the easiest conversations to have because almost everyone is a consumer of video. Most businesses simply get it. The piece missing from the puzzle for most companies is the "Chief Streaming Officer" who becomes responsible for executing these opportunities. My hope is that this book will spur more people to consider this position inside their company. I'm happy to report that I am now connected to multiple "Chief Streaming Officers" on LinkedIN. I think it's a trend! Not a fad.

Paul Richards
Chief Streaming Officer
PTZOptics • Moravian College
Greater Philadelphia Area • 500+

Chapter 7: A Home Run was Hit!

So I can't say that I knew exactly when it was going to happen, but I knew that when you are creating this much video, you are bound to catch a break and something is going to go viral. To use a baseball metaphor, we would hit singles all the time, we hit multiple doubles, a couple triples and at least one homerun every year. The doubles and triples happen to be live tutorial videos that were starting to reach 50,000 and 100,000 views on YouTube. These videos were really starting to garner attention and help our channel gain valuable subscribers. The home run video was titled "How to Engage Your Audience By Using Multiple Cameras" and I guess it hit all the right signals inside the YouTube algorithm.

How to Engage Your Audience By Using Multiple Cameras
PTZOptics
Subscribed 6.7K
433,369 views
Add to Share ••• More 34 20

This video currently has over 400,000 views and I believe it has a lot to do with the viewer retention. The video is 5 minutes long and according to YouTube analytics the average viewer retention is roughly 50%. If we go back to our statistics from Salesforce.com this would buy us 46 salespeople working for us for over a month. The real world response was incredible. The particular camera model demonstrated in this video sold out immediately. The regular camera sales rates were exceeded that month by over 20 times the normal sell through.

We did a couple things to tip the scales with this video including advertising to the correct demographics upfront. I will go over our marketing approach in the next chapter but the takeaway is that if you keep swinging for the fences you are bound to hit a home run sooner or later. This video—which did exceedingly well—also helped boost other videos published around the same time. We had spikes in our normal YouTube viewership when this video was really kicking. It helped launch other key videos into the 100K view mark. It was a really fun time to see our work recognized on both YouTube and on the phones. Our sales team took immediate notice. Everyone from operations to manufacturing started to take notice. Finally our Director of Operations was more interested in planning our marketing initiatives more closely with the company's product stocking plans.

Chapter 8: Our Approach to Marketing

When it comes to social media and content creation, it's all about creativity. Personally, I have found that pushing the boundaries of what we could do technically speaking helps me uncover our next "Creative Hack," When I can spot a new workflow or time saver, this is the perfect opportunity to create a tutorial video. Being an innovator does comes at a cost. Even to this day, we are making mistakes and breaking things, but I wouldn't want it any other way.

So how do we grow from here?

The StreamGeeks have a fully equipped video production studio and a team of trained professionals ready to capitalize on the next live streaming breakthrough. Well, that's where this book really begins. In order to grow and succeed, we really need to get creative with our growth hacks. So let me share the tools and technology that have made the biggest difference for us over the past three years.

First and foremost, generating awareness for our company has been the number one goal. Finding a balance between what I personally find exciting and what actually makes sense from a business standpoint is where we spend most of our time. Our long term strategy is to create lasting relationships with people from around the world who value our work. The modern business is more than just a product or service. Businesses need to provide value above and beyond their core revenue generators. This process should be both fun and rewarding.

So here is the backbone of our strategy. It's called inbound marketing. Essentially we want to turn strangers into leads for our business and a relatively easy way to do this is offering gated content. Gated content and inbound marketing have been around for a long time. Surely you have seen the "free ebooks" and "downloadable checklists" available in return for your contact information. Assuming that this is done right, you can build up large databases of leads for your business. Inbound marketing then allows us to nurture these leads intelligently based on their interests.

Have you ever heard that marketers ruin everything? That's because every chance they get marketers are trying to generate leads. Landing pages and traditional gated content definitely still work. The more value you are offering, the more likely your leads will take the next step in your marketing funnel. We look at things a little differently than most traditional marketers. We have found that integrating our inbound offers into a larger live video presentation, provides us a chance to deliver the ultimate offer. What's the ultimate offer? It's an invitation to your community. Sure, we are still creating gated content but what we really want is an engaged community of customers. Live video promotes viewer engagement like no other medium.

Inbound marketing may seem simple but it definitely takes some upfront planning. The most important tip I can give is requiring that leads submit information about their persona. A persona is the type of business or job position that the contact should be categorized in. Eventually when you find yourself with thousands of inbound leads, your most useful tool is intelligent organization. The persona guides your team to decide how they should interact with each bucket of contacts. We have recently published an hour long webinar with HubSpot, one of the leading inbound marketing platforms. It's now available for on-demand viewing on our YouTube and Facebook channel. In this webinar, we explain in detail how having an inbound marketing plan is an essential tool for our growth strategy.

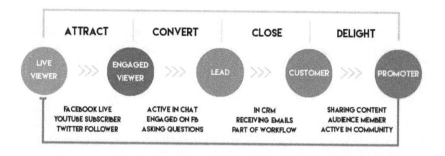

The next key to our growth has always been excitement and creativity. One of the most empowering emotions I feel about our new StreamGeeks office is the open opportunity for the future. You simply cannot produce great content in a place that doesn't feel positive. At our previous office, we were constantly brushing up against disgruntled sales people who didn't understand our marketing process. Creativity is a beautiful thing but the flame for a good idea can be blown out quickly by negativity. If you want to be successful, do whatever it takes to find your creative zone and protect it against distractions. In our old office, some of the confrontation with other coworkers about our content was productive. Even when it wasn't the most constructive criticism, our small team was often able to use the energy in our creativity walks. Good or bad we would come up with a new idea that would push us even further. So whatever circumstance you are in, find a way to take your surroundings and make a way for your creative inner self to succeed.

The StreamGeeks live streaming workflow has been designed to optimize show attendance. We deliver value via video and scale our reach using social media advertising. The team uses HubSpot to organize inbound leads and notify targeted personas with tailored email notifications. This way we know the content is specifically interesting to our email recipients. Our process leverages the massive audiences available on Facebook and YouTube and takes advantage of platforms prioritization of live video content.

Like all good marketers, the StreamGeeks always start campaigns with the best possible content. We specifically make our target customer demographics and personas. The team will routinely brainstorm using the latest core inbound marketing strategies as a guiding principle for content creation. One thing we have started to consider more in our marketing strategy is where the content fits into an overall sales funnel. The StreamGeeks team is always crafting live video content to support each stage of the inbound marketing sales funnel. It's easy to get caught up in the attract stage, when you are focusing on generating new leads. But as you grow you will find it's more beneficial to spend time converting and closing existing leads already in your CRM. It's actually easier to convert customers with content geared toward contacts who are already aware of your core offerings. The contacts who have already opted in are often the lowest hanging fruit.

So we have a strategy to build our business with inbound marketing. Our process for creativity is to remain interested and excited about the content we are producing. But when did it all come together? What was the technology that enabled us? What were the game changers in terms of hardware and software? The next few chapters will delve into our live streaming system piece by piece. Hopefully this book will save you time and money when it comes to selecting solutions for your own live production system. But first let's acknowledge the most important part of live streaming. That's where all the magic happens.

Chapter 9: Where the Magic Happens

I created a classic Venn diagram in a recent presentation to outline exactly where the magic of live streaming takes place. It happens to be the bridge between your business and your community. Your business being your spokesperson with your on screen talent or the personality you have representing your brand. Your community is your audience made up of strangers, customers, and prospects who are interested in what you have to offer.

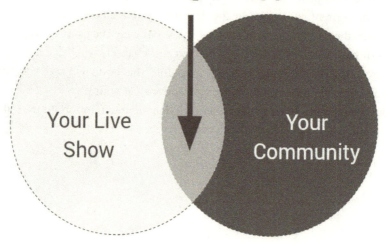

This is the space where your company has the chance to answer questions from your community. This is the bridge of potential that connects your best intended value with the real people who are taking time out of their day. Often viewers only have a few minutes to see if your offer is either educational or entertaining. The best presentations are both educational and entertaining, of course. Entertaining your audience while you provide value should be considered a high skill. This is the magic we should always strive for.

MARKETING TIP

Don't be afraid of giving away too much information. Your goal should be to deliver as much value as possible. Your reward will be your audience and the connections you make with the people actually need your products/services.

Our best shows start with a premise that sounds both entertaining and educational. Most of our audience will tune in regularly for the educational portion of our shows. In many cases viewers can justify the time taken away from other tasks, knowing that the free education takes precedence over other opportunities. Making an honest effort to provide educational value is a rewarding process.

Not only are our viewers happy but it allows our entire team and audience to grow closer. Learning can be personal but it can also be a very communal experience. When our audience starts to comment with information that adds significant value to the conversation, we know we're on the way to a good show.

Once the value has been delivered in a professional manner, it's okay to break up the course material with some entertaining moments. For us this usually means a moment to make fun of ourselves or acknowledge a funny comment in the chat room. Some shows we plant a few funny jokes into our agenda but on the whole our content is geared toward professional education.

Somewhere along the line we got the idea to save the chat room transcripts. I would use these to review questions asked during the live show. Having these handy greatly helps when writing the blog post articles that go along with each video. Reading through the chat transcripts helped me realize that we had finally hit a point in our community's growth where we could crowdsource ideas with relative ease. This is a sweet reward for our hard work and a tipping point many successful creators enjoy. The ability to read through the comments and come up with our next idea is mind blowing. Every week we can pick through a list of recommendations and choose the topic that seems the most fun or has the most support behind it. Because the comments are custom tailored to our latest presentation, crowdsourcing content topics is a game changer for our business.

Chapter 10: LinkedIn Live Streaming

LinkedIn has recently announced a new feature for the business-focused social media platform.... That's right Live Streaming. As of early February 2019, LinkedIn will be rolling out Live Streaming as an invite-only BETA feature for USA users. If you haven't already been invited to be part of the LinkedIN Live roll for the invite-only beta phase, you will be able to apply for access to the service in the coming months.

So, how are businesses, brands, and individuals going to start using LinkedIn Live? Well, LinkedIn has stated that they hope users will broadcast content that falls in line with the business-related content that is already popular on the platform. This could include live conferences, product announcements, Q&A sessions, and other office hours events. On a scale from Facebook Selfie Streams to LinkedIn Live content, you can bet that LinkedIN live streams will make a name for itself by catering toward business-related interests. So here are ten tips to consider how you can be successful live streaming on LinkedIn.

1. First of all, plan to create specific content for LinkedIN. It would be a mistake to live stream the same content you are planning for YouTube and Facebook to LinkedIn. I know that time is money so perhaps consider creating a custom introduction on LinkedIn that

leads to your main content that is streamed to other platforms as well. One of the best tips we have learned about live streaming over the past 5 years is the power of creating platform-specific content. Everyone knows that LinkedIn members moderate the content they find on their newsfeed. If your content is not business related you are sure to hear about it in the comments. Listen to the feedback you get in your contents comments and always strive to improve your approach based on user feedback.

2. LinkedIn is known as an online resume for business professionals and the most likely viewers of your LinkedIn live streams will be your professional connections. This network includes your co-workers, people you used to work with and prospective clients. With this in mind, your LinkedIn live streams should remain professional and business oriented. Strive to create presentations in a professional space that properly reflects who you are and the business you represent.

3. If you are used to live streaming on YouTube and Facebook, you are going to have a huge leg up on your competition when it comes to preparing to go live. If you are waiting for access to LinkedIn Live (the feature is currently in BETA at the time of publishing this book), consider using Facebook and YouTube as a practice space. While you may have had success with a laid-back, impromptu live stream on traditional social media platforms, you will want to put your best foot forward on a platform like LinkedIn. Think about preparing for a LinkedIn live session the same way that you would for a professional interview.

4. Respect the rules that LinkedIn has posted about live streaming. LinkedIn for example requests that all live streams be above 10 minutes to give users time to find your stream and engage with the online audience. You should know that Facebook and YouTube have their own rules as well. If you have broken some of Facebook or YouTube's guidelines without repercussions in the past don't expect to get away with breaking the rules on LinkedIn. With a platform as powerful as LinkedIn for live streaming, you don't want to have your live streaming privileges revoked.

5. LinkedIn is a place where users highly regard their profile accuracy and business reputation. Unlike, YouTube and Facebook which suffers from large amounts of fake accounts and sometimes unaccountable activity, LinkedIn's community and established culture will lead to a higher level of quality and accountability. With this in mind, you want to make sure that your content is highly produced and effective in telling your story in a professional way.

Remember, time is money and the users on LinkedIn are all aware of that as business professionals.

6. Short videos are already performing extremely well on the LinkedIn platform. Facebook has publicly stated that viewers on the platform spend on average up to 3 times more time watching live content versus pre-recorded on-demand videos. With this in mind, consider how you can incorporate live viewer engagement on your LinkedIn live streams. Do not make the mistake of ignoring your live audience. Another new rule from LinkedIn is that users are not encouraged to play recorded content during a live stream. Consider addressing live comments and recognizing your audience by name. Remember that the people commenting on your LinkedIn live stream are part of your business network and may be important partners and/or prospects for your business.

7. When was the last time that you updated your LinkedIn profile page? When you go live on the platform, consider keeping your branding consistent. LinkedIn Live streaming is available for both individuals and business pages. You should keep your business page, updated and consistent with your companies branding. Your personal live streams should be no different. Consider your ability to share live streams with relevant business pages, groups, and like-minded individuals. It's time to take LinkedIn off the back burner and schedule a meeting with your social media team to think about how you can take full advantage of the platform.

8. If your company is not prepared to create professional live video content that is in line with your corporate branding, consider creating a dedicated space in your office for this purpose. As you can see in our live streaming studio, we have the ability to live stream to YouTube for professional webinars, Facebook to dedicated social media related content, and LinkedIn for professional business updates. An investment in live streaming equipment is an investment in your entire business. From sales to marketing, and beyond, don't get left behind as the final social media giant LinkedIn joins Facebook, YouTube, Instagram and Amazon.

9. So where do you go from here? If you are thinking about building a live streaming studio in your office, this book should help you stimulate the ideas you need to be thinking about.

10. Have fun. And enjoy your success.

Chapter 11: Live Product Presentations

Now that Amazon is allowing merchants to live stream on their platform. Whether you want to use LinkedIn for B2B or Amazon for B2C, live streaming a product/service presentation is become more and more powerful. Have you ever watched one of the live product announcements from Apple, Facebook or Google online? These events have the ability to capture viewers' attention with the latest product releases in a setting that is live, interactive, and exciting!

While most businesses don't have the clout or financial resources as let's say Apple... everyone now has access to live streaming in the connected world of online social media. You can leverage Facebook, YouTube or Twitch to reach your audience with live streaming and hosting a live product demonstration can create massive results to further your businesses marketing and sales initiatives. LinkedIn has recently announced that they will now offer live streaming for both personal profiles and business pages creating the ideal venue for many B2B businesses. Amazon has also announced that live streaming is now available for select merchants on their e-commerce platform.

With the world moving toward visually stimulating, and interactive communication, we thought the time was ripe to share some of our tips and tricks for hosting amazing product demonstrations. Not to mention the latest statistics saying that viewers find live streams 80% more appealing than blogs and consumers are 67% more likely to buy a product seen on a live stream.

Over the past 4 years, our company has literally hosted thousands of live events. We started with boring webinars and struggled to gain traction... We found that live stream on both YouTube and Facebook simultaneously gained us 10X the number of viewers versus traditional webinars. We found our audience was more engaged and excited to be part of an online broadcast versus a two-way video conference style webinar. By reducing the barriers to entry, which traditionally included downloading a webinar software, and registering for an event, we have found that our live broadcast attendance has sky-rocketed and our product demonstrations are much more interactive.

The first most important tip for hosting a successful live product demonstration is authenticity. Gone are the days when businesses can simply post a perfect video of their product and company where nothing could ever go wrong. Today customers want to see what really "comes in the box" and you will notice that audiences want to connect to real people whom they can relate with. Did you know Facebook reports that on average viewers will watch 3-8 times longer when a video is live versus pre-recorded?

The concept is the same whether you sell services or physical products. It's time to leverage the power of live product demonstrations to connect with customers in multiple stages in your sales funnel. Speaking of your sales funnel... Live product demonstrations can be used to attract new leads and delight existing customers but most importantly it can shorten your overall sales cycle. Nothing is better than a customer testimonial shown on your live stream in front of a group of interested prospects. This is called social proof, and it is one of the most authentic and powerful ways to connect with your audience.

Whether you are planning a new product release or a deep-dive new feature overview, live streaming can be used to deepen your connection with your prospects and customers alike. So where do you get started? First of all, you might want to consider subscribing to our YouTube channel... We have a free guide available at ptzoptics.com/demo which will walk you through our process for creating visually stimulating live product demonstrations.

We have found that magic happens when your presentation is both informative and entertaining. Think about live streaming as a real-time bridge between your company and your online community. Remember that everyone in your chat room is a real person and if you present a compelling call to action they will be likely to take that next step. We have found that many of the comments in our live stream chat room turn into new ideas for show topics.

Since all of these chats are saved to your videos, they are easy to review with your sales and marketing teams after the broadcast. Once you establish your business as an industry thought leader you may find that you can crowd-source new ideas and customer feature requests that will keep your company ahead of the curve.

So we get it. Live product demonstrations are a powerful tool for sales and marketing. But where do we get started?

Okay, here are some tips to start thinking about. In our downloadable guide, you can dig even further into these topics.

1. Do you have a presentation that properly reflects your brand? You may want to consider building a dedicated space in your office where you can create videos and product demonstration with good lighting and ample space for your products.
2. Do you have a brand spokesperson? Is there someone in your organization willing to get on camera and make live product demonstrations...
3. The two camera production trick. If you have physical products, it's important to be able to show you're a close-up view of your product. With at least two cameras you can transition between a view of your presenter and close up view of your products. While you are on a close-up view of your products you presenter can read detailed information from a data sheet or manual and your audience will never know
4. What about a highly professional presentation? Where you don't want to mess up a single word... Consider using a Teleprompter like the one we have here. You can create a script or a simple checklist of bullet points for your talent to read during the live presentation
5. Also, you should think about your video production workflow. Live streaming technology has come a long way in the past couple of years. Everyone is trying to make their software more intuitive

and easy enough for a beginner to get the hang of things quickly.
Do you have someone who can be a producer? This person can
also moderate the chat room and display valuable social proof
during the live stream…

Chapter 12: Working with Local Business

So let me start by saying that the StreamGeeks are extremely lucky to have a company that benefits from the exposure we provide. In essence, part of our job is to look for new markets and businesses that can use live streaming technology. Our best content comes from proof of concept videos that we use as case studies. As storytellers, we need a story to tell and I have found that there is no substitute for hands on learning. Luckily almost any business can benefit from online exposure with live streaming.

The first company we worked with was called, Old Soul Decor. The small business owner, Krystal Reinhard, was happy to invite us in and capture her new line of jewelry and decor on video. I had the idea to present her jewelry in a "QVC style" layout. Getting to know business owners like this really helps our team understand what it's like out in the real world. I remember

MARKETING TIP

Creating a "QVC Style" television broadcast may be easier than you think. You can download a free template to get started with Adobe Photoshop at

https://ptzoptics.com/land-ing/QVC-style.html

Krystal saying, "We all know we need to be live streaming, but it's just so hard to find the time."

The opportunity to create a television style broadcast for a small business, on the same block as our office, was just incredible. The content was absolute gold for StreamGeeks and PTZOptics—our camera brand company. We live streamed the event to Krystal's Facebook page and the broadcast attracted roughly 15-30 simultaneous viewers. The entire broadcast was roughly one hour long. Our total reach was almost 2,000 people. We checked in with Krystal a few weeks after the show to learn more about the impact for her business.

Krystal told us that she did in fact close a few sales as a result of the live stream. She also received multiple inquiries and phone calls from others who directly referenced the live video they had seen. It was great to hear that our efforts made a direct impact on her business. The whole show opened up our eyes to how many other businesses we can start helping. Like many other businesses, Krystal has a Facebook page which she has been managing since she started the company. But I was surprised to find out that she did not have a YouTube channel. Luckily, I did record the entire one hour broadcast and suggested that she use it. Businesses with no content can upload a broadcast like this in smaller chunks to jump start their YouTube channels when time allows.

At the time that I am writing this book, we are in the midst of planning multiple case studies explaining the power of live streaming to staple local business types. We are working with a car dealership to pitch their latest cars on Facebook Live. This concept is one of my favorites because we are able to start a live broadcast from the showroom floor and transition into a live test drive. We can transition back and forth from a mobile broadcast on the road and the showroom floor using a cellular bonding technology (the LiveU Solo) and a cloud based video production software called EasyLive.

We are also hoping to help out local restaurants and share how live streaming the preparation of their tasty dishes can increase business. It's one thing to tell businesses what they can achieve, but it's another thing to show them. The ultimate goal of StreamGeeks is to show the world what is possible. Working with local businesses from all walks of life helps us break through the early adoption stages of streaming media.

Michael, our producer, suggested nicely that we start with "camera ready" locations. This makes a lot of sense in the wide open world of small business. Old Soul Decor was a beautiful boutique with a very passionate owner willing to get on camera. We are in the process of choosing businesses that will exemplify the absolute best proof of concepts in their respective industries. It's going to be a fun ride.

Chapter 13: Facebook: it Works!

Before we jump into the hardware. I have to say that I think Facebook was the big game changer for us. When I first started live streaming, YouTube was our main live streaming destination. I was so comfortable on YouTube that I neglected to stream to Facebook early on. This was a big mistake because I missed the "First Mover Advantage." Credit for cultivating our Facebook presence goes 100% to Tess, our social media manager. I was doubtful about how much actual business could be derived from Facebook. Boy was I wrong!

There are a couple amazing things about Facebook that make the platform superior to other social media sites. First of all, Facebook has the world's attention. People go there because they are bored and they often end up watching some video they had no idea existed. This makes Facebook the ideal place to attract new customers who aren't going out of their way to search for you. YouTube works in the exact opposite. YouTube is a search engine that delivers to people exactly what they are searching for. So combining our marketing efforts on both YouTube and Facebook really doubled our effective reach. Facebook was sending us new traffic based on our target demographics and YouTube was doing great using keywords.

The first thing you have to do to be effective on Facebook is understand the importance of engagement. If our entire goal is to turn strangers into customers, we need to think about engaging strangers. We found that forming a Facebook User Group was perhaps the biggest hack on the platform. We always advertised our videos, but advertising a user group invitation is different. Facebook has the most powerful demographic targeting available on any marketing platform. One marketer I talked to told me you can find "mothers with newborns living in Nebraska" and it's true. Facebook knows a lot about its users. When you start using their marketing platform, all of that information comes out. It's a little scary.

I have to say, with a somewhat guilty smile on my face, that we used FOMO. FOMO is short for "Fear of Missing Out." We often promote a post that says "Have You Joined Yet? 100's of other live streamers are collaborating right here, right now." Boosting a post like this is extremely effective for us because it beckons the question. What am I potentially missing out on? Once we have contacts join our group we basically get free advertising in their newsfeeds. When you join a Facebook Group you are essentially telling Facebook that this is a source of media that you are very interested in. So Facebook regularly shows popular posts from the group in users news feeds free of charge.

But to be fair, our Facebook User Group is everything we hoped and dreamed it would be. It's the first place I turn to when I want advice or feedback on a new show idea. It's also a place that I often search through to find a customer picture or project for an upcoming campaign. The User Group makes the process of getting to know our power users and most valiant supporters easier. At this point, Tess and I know all of the most active User Group members. Most of them are regular viewers of our show.

Chapter 14: The Technology Game Changers

So the very first product we bought when we decided to get serious about live streaming was a custom-built Windows 7 computer from Tom Sinclair of Eastern Shore Broadcasting. Up until this point, I was actually using my Dell laptop with a couple cameras connected via USB. We had Tom build us the fastest computer possible capable of eight camera inputs and enough horsepower to stream, record, and host video callers from around the world. The specifications for this beast PC are outlined on our website. It stands at four rack units tall and has been the core workhorse behind hundreds of live streams and thousands of short videos that we have produced over the past three years.

CAMERA SWITCHING TIP

Most professionals will always use simple cuts between camera shots. Using too many fancy transitions can actually make your production look cheesy. Only use fancy transitions like a stinger or cube zoom when you are changing media types.

Producing content live is so powerful because it eliminates the need for post-production. Almost everything we do is produced live. We have a process and we have the equipment necessary. Once you understand a live video production workflow, it can be contagious to think that everything can be produced live in a single take. The equipment you will need to produce video like this will be entirely dependent on the content you want to make. Would an over the shoulder camera make your interviews look more professional? Could a ceiling camera give viewers a better perspective of your workspace? Each camera angle has the power to transport your audience into a new learning space. Switching between cameras is the oldest trick in the book when it comes to holding viewers' attention. The best thing you can do to separate your content from the rest of the world, is increase your storytelling capability. So instead of talking about products and specifications, I want to share with you a few real world case studies from our studio in terms of storytelling.

We have eight cameras in our studio and each is used for a different purpose. In an ideal video production, we want to give our viewers as many camera angles as possible without using them just because we can. Each camera transition has to be part of our storytelling process. To get this right, you have to have good communication between your talent and your producer. Teamwork is key here and reviewing your recorded video together is a great way to analyze what worked and what could be improved. As I mentioned in our first studio, we have tally lights that light up next to a given camera. This is a live notification showing the talent which camera they should be looking at.

Let's start with the two camera classic layout. Camera one and two are the show staples and they provide our main introductory video angles. Camera one is focused on our main presentation area. Camera two is a PTZ (Pan, Tilt and Zoom) camera that is used to transition in between zoomed in close up shots during our presentation. Since everything is shot in real time, when we

COMPUTER TIP

If you are using your laptop to live stream your show check out your settings. See if your power settings are set to "high performance". Also, check and make sure your graphics card is enabled with the program you are running.

transition between each camera the audience doesn't miss a beat. You will notice that professional television broadcasters always use quick cuts between cameras. We have found that the fancier stinger transitions only work well when you are transitioning between different types of media such as a presentation deck or b-roll video clips.

Most PTZ cameras will usually have multiple preset positions saved. For example, we can use these presets to show a presenter full screen or a camera wide shot. We can use this camera to zoom in on a particularly interesting product on the table during a live demonstration. If you can only afford to start with two cameras this is one of the most effective systems because you can transition back and forth between both cameras. In this manner you can create hundreds of different angles live. The PTZ camera is used to line up with your next close up while your main camera is always ready for you when you need it. This setup gives your production tons of great detail and dimension.

My personal favorite camera shot is the behind the scenes wide angle cameras we have placed behind our producer. We also have one behind our main presentation area. Yes, these are the same cameras from our Home Run video. These wide angle cameras allow us to get up close and personal during the broadcast. They also allow us to turn around and address our audience in a way that furthers our storytelling capabilities. When used properly, our over the shoulder cameras draw our audience into a new segment that is personal. This transitions the content into the heart of our offer. Wide angle cameras are great for capturing detailed focus on a certain area and blurring out the background. In photography, the blurry background is often referred to as Bokeh. So we have our wide angle camera cameras set to focus in on a particular area and blur out the rest of our studio which creates a live artistic dimension to our broadcasts.

My second favorite camera is the ceiling camera looking down at our presentation table. This camera angle is used in almost every major webinar that we produce. We almost always have some product or physical representation of our content that is able to enhance the conversation. Viewers want to see exactly what it is that we are presenting. Sharing an overhead view is often a well appreciated perspective. We use a PTZ camera here as well. This allows us to save multiple preset positions for various items on our table. This camera angle is amazing for presentations and I love using live Telestration ink over this video feed. When I am explaining a product or floor plan we use the NewTek NDI Telestrator to digitally draw on the video. This really brings the audience into a specific area of attention. In this way the camera provides a classroom like feel to our presentation.

Finally, the extra cameras we have are for our "sister set." We have two set areas in our studio and they are setup side by side. This allows us to quickly move from one set to the next for different segments in our show.

It also allows us to use the cameras from opposing sets to gain extra angled shots of our presenters. Placing cameras five to ten feet away from the presentation center wall can provide interesting angles that you often see on TV. A 30-45 degree angle from the center of your presenters main focus can really add production value to your presentation. We like to use these angles as an opportunity to display a lower third title and reinforce our presentation quality early on in our broadcast.

All of our cameras are controlled with a video production software called vMix. I have been a fan of vMix from the very first time I used it. I find the controls intuitive and I love a software that is essentially endless with its potential possibilities. I have an entire course on the software you can take for free which is available on UDEMY. So for this book, I will simply be explaining how we use it and why. Now that we have a dedicated producer, Michael uses vMix to control all of our PTZ cameras. Even though he has a physical IP joystick controller, Michael finds that keeping all the video production and camera control in one location allows him to be more productive.

So if you have never seen vMix before ... imagine a computer screen with two squares. The right square is what you are live streaming or recording. The left square is your preview screen where you que up a video ready to transition into your next shot. Below these two squares are rows of more squares. This is where you organize everything your broadcast will have access to. These can be video clips, pictures, more cameras, audio sources and other media. I love the layout and our video producer's main job is switching between the available squares we have saved into our show preset. Everything is just a click away in vMix and you will find that users absolutely love this software. I should note that vMix is only available in Windows and there are many other equally easy to use software offerings available. In fact, I also offer free courses on Wirecast and OBS you can take to learn more about these as well. No matter which live streaming software you end up using, the strategies we talk about in this book can apply to your workflow.

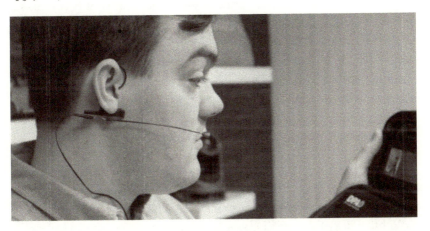

In the audio realm, the next game changer for us was the DPA D: Fine headset microphone. These are the most expensive microphones in the industry. So be aware, these are not cheap! These headset microphones are so well made that they have helped us overcome many other audio mistakes simply because they output such a high quality signal to our audio mixer. When you have an issue with your audio, it's best to think about things in a chain. If your microphone is not good quality, it's going to be near impossible to fix it downstream. Upgrading your microphones will affect what you can actually do with your audio mixer to improve the overall sound quality.

We have made every mistake in the book when it comes to audio. So here are some tips about what I have learned. First of all, you have to check your audio before you go live. If you plan on bringing in multiple guests, check their audio before the show as well. Nothing is worse than bad audio. If you can afford really good microphones like the DPA D: Fine headsets, then buy them! It's incredibly hard to solve audio problems because there are often so many variables. Knowing that you have good quality microphones eliminates at least one important variable when you are trying to troubleshoot an audio issue.

Headset microphones are my favorite type because they stay where they need to be and they usually have little interference. Lapel microphones work when they are setup correctly but they often battle with ruffled shirts and bad placement. Headsets are almost always placed in an ideal position. They capture 99% of conversations no matter which way your talent turns their head. Another piece of advice I would offer is going wireless. We purchased the Shure BLX wireless combo microphone systems and absolutely love it. Now I do wish that we purchased the ULX systems with a longer range. Going wireless really allows us as creators to have the freedom to move around. For the longest time we were using hardwired microphones which literally tethered us to a single location. If you want your talent to have the ability to move around, go wireless. It feels great!

Now we have briefly covered all the cameras and microphones that we use in the StreamGeeks studio. Here's the next big tip. Learn how to use Adobe After Effects and Photoshop. We use the programs almost every day. With the use of a shared Dropbox account our team can quickly and easily update and manage the graphics for our weekly show. Some of the content we create such as an intro video or outro segment can be reused over and over again. You may even want to outsource the creation of this work online with a freelancer. Whatever you end up doing, your show graphics will likely come from some Adobe Creative Product.

I highly suggest creating custom made titles and lower thirds which can be loaded into your live streaming software. No matter what software you are using, you should have the ability to change the text for different shows and guests without the need of photoshop. So you may find that After Effects and Photoshop are only required for the setup of your show and not necessarily used in your day-to-day video production. We use Photoshop almost every day because we are constantly branding and customizing our content.

If you work with a team, you should consider using a shared Dropbox folder to manage your show content. You can have a folder for images, videos, audio, and other files which everyone can reference. In fact, if you reference a file in your video production software and change it on another computer using Dropbox, the file will actually be updated in your live show without having to touch anything. So outlining the graphics you need and referencing them in your live streaming software can make your entire workflow seamless. Remotely updating files really makes teamwork easy.

Our normal show starts with a brief introduction, followed by an intro clip and our prepared presentation. But your show could be almost any format. I would suggest drawing inspiration from your favorite shows and watching other live streamers. It becomes a game of sorts when we start to wonder how other live shows are being produced. I still remember a small project where I tried to copy the look and feel of a CNN show. Now you can find pre-made show templates available on Videohive.net and other custom resellers for almost any show type. I always start a show by shopping on Videohive and looking for a custom After Effects template that I can adopt for our show theme. Sometimes I choose a mixture of multiple templates and only take the parts and pieces that I need from each. The amount of customizable templates available for Adobe After Effects and Photoshop today is astounding!

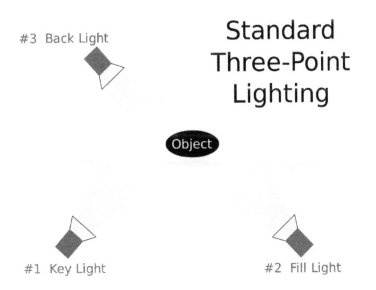

Finally, one of the biggest upgrades we made in our studio was lighting. Good lighting is very noticeable. We have been trained to expect good lighting from watching television. The easiest way to ensure good lighting is the "Three-Point" lighting system. This best practice consists of a Key light, a Fill light, and a Backlight. I found that each subject may need three point lighting. Since we usually have two hosts, I need four or five lights in-order to achieve good three point lighting. The Key and Fill lights provide your subject with even lighting. The Backlight provides a "halo" effect around your subjects outline. This is my personal favorite light. The Backlight is often overlooked but it makes the most difference. This light really makes your subject "pop" off of the background.

The easiest way to get started with lighting is to buy an LED light kit. Three to five lights should be enough to get started. LED lights are great because they don't get hot like traditional tungsten or fluorescent lights. LED lights also have great CRI (Color Rendering Indexes). LED lights are usually available in either daylight or bi-color. We always suggest bi-color because this gives you a knob to turn which can adjust the light color temperature. There is a process for color matching your cameras and the light that is on your subjects. Often women want to have a warm light and men like a cooler blue.

Chapter 15: Our SEO & Growth Hacking Strategies

The StreamGeeks have already published some really great content on growth hacking your way through Facebook Live and YouTube. But I wanted to share some of our tried and true SEO practices that we use to promote our company. First of all, almost all of our content is made to support our larger "Blue Ocean Strategy." The blue ocean strategy originally pioneered by authors, W. Chan Kim and Renée Mauborgne, is essentially the process of finding a space in the market where you can innovate. Instead of trying to compete with everyone else in a competitive landscape, it's ultimately more effective to carve out your own niche. It's in the space that you can innovate where you can become the leader.

So as we create content, we are paving our own path toward a goal of industry thought leadership and innovation. Sure, our goal is to maximize exposure but at the same time we are hacking our way through a very competitive landscape. We want to build a pathway to our brand that leads the right type of people to our door. It is possible to come up with a one hit wonder, but it's much more likely that we will have to tackle one topic at a time. In fact, HubSpot has recently released a very compelling search engine optimization study suggesting that clusters of related topics can help support what they call pillar content. They suggest that brands should focus on a set number of content pillars supported by clusters of content which deliver more detailed information. The idea of "Topic Clusters" is to create content that supports an overall strategy that intelligently links everything together.

Thinking in terms of content creation strategy, we now understand how to create high quality video content to support our initiatives. So curating the content topics and long term strategies to support our content pillars has become our focus. The actual video content is often the centerpiece for our work and I will explain how we take that content and optimize the delivery for search engines like Google and Bing.

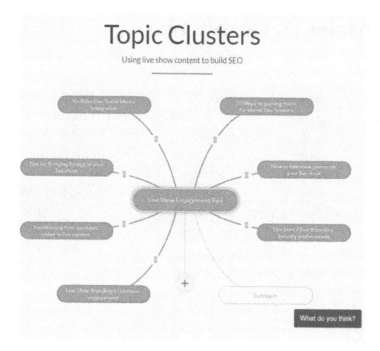

First of all, good video content starts with topic research. To start, we always create an agenda. The agenda itself is a great starting point for writing the blog post. The blog posts are incredibly important, as they are the core of our searchable content on Google. I start by going back to the recorded video and taking snapshots of the most important segments. These pictures become the image content we use on social media and throughout the blog posts. Google likes to see all sorts of related media content inside your blog post. Every couple paragraphs of text should generally have a picture or video to break things up. Video is an important factor but everything else including images, text, and subject relevance is just as important. The blog posts are where all the media comes together. Uploading high quality images with files named as the keywords you are going for is a great tip. Because we name our picture files with the keywords we are going after, our picture files dominate on Google Pictures.

Google is now searching much deeper into your content than simple keywords and search phrases. While good titles are still important, Google is trying to predict the intent of its users and deliver the most relevant website results possible. So whenever we publish a video, it always includes a detailed blog post with images, embedded videos, related articles, and detailed written information. An easy way to start blogging about your video is to take each picture/snapshot from your video that you have collected and explain what is happening at that point in your video. For a normal 10-20 minute video, I will take roughly 4-6 pictures and post them through my article. Each picture will help me explain my 6-8 paragraph blog post and the content becomes incredibly SEO friendly. When I am done with my blog post, I go back to my YouTube video and paste in a couple relevant paragraphs into the YouTube description. Let's not forget that YouTube is the world's second largest search engine.

One of the wonderful benefits of live streaming is the organic reach and long term video ranking capabilities. When a normal video is uploaded to YouTube it has to accumulate views and watch time starting at zero. Watch time is one of the most important factors that YouTube uses to rank videos. Once you have an audience willing to tune in to your broadcasts, you will be accumulating views and watch time during your live stream. Facebook has reported that viewers will spend three times as much time watching live video versus pre-recorded content. As soon as your video is available on-demand on either YouTube or Facebook it will have a huge boost over regular uploaded content. All the watch time you have accumulated during the live broadcast will automatically be attributed to your video.

So if you haven't noticed, the key to SEO is creating content in many different formats. Our live show has become the starting point for our content creation whether it be a written blog post, pictures and actual video creation. There are a couple additional types of media you can produce from your live show that we have found helpful.

One type of content that might not be so obvious is a podcast. You can export the audio for a podcast simply by downloading an audio only copy of your video. We have found that this does work to some extent. There are some strategies you can use during your live stream if you are definitely going to use the audio content for a podcast. One strategy you can use is simply remembering not to reference anything visual. The last thing your podcast listeners want to hear about is something that only you can see. Ultimately we have found that recording a dedicated podcast is the best approach. Roughly one hour before each show we will sit down and record the audio only podcast version of our show. This prepares the team for the live show and provides a fun prep time space for us to digest the content for the upcoming live show.

Finally, we almost always send out press releases for our popular live shows. Press releases are an interesting tool that still work today. We often get inquiries from our press releases that turn into real business opportunities. One of the great things about online press releases is that you can embed your video into the release even if it's scheduled to happen in the future. We often write about the subject of our show and mention our live giveaway. We leave press release readers with an embedded copy of our video. These press releases can circulate all throughout the internet and authors from news agencies may decide to write about your show. It's definitely a worthwhile exercise for our most important live shows.

Chapter 16: Video Marketing, YouTube vs Facebook

MARKETING TIP

Try creating custom Facebook and YouTube outro clips. You can include your best call to actions and insert them into the end of each video you create.

YouTube and Facebook are the world's largest platforms for advertising video today. It's interesting to think about how different the Red and Blue giants have become. Facebook is the world's largest social media network and YouTube is the world's second largest search engine. As online video continues to dominate the internet, Google predicts that video will represent 80% of all internet traffic by 2020.

YouTube's approach to delivering video is based on what users are searching for. As a search engine, YouTube's algorithm uses its database of video and user preferences to deliver the most relevant content for users. Google has publicly stated that the algorithm is trying to predict the searchers intent. Therefore YouTube's algorithm is designed to deliver the highest quality content possible based on everything they know about the user habits and their current search phrase. How YouTube determines what the search engine delivers is an incredibly complicated equation that is purposely left mysterious by Google. Most experts agree that video watch time and search phrase relevance are the two most important video ranking attributes. YouTube wants to keep viewers on the platform for as long as possible. If a video is keeping audiences engaged for long periods of time, this signals to the algorithm that the viewer queries are relevant to this content. These signals can make a video go viral or keep it from being suggested to other users.

MARKETING TIP

Try Facebook's advertising audience option "Page Likes and their friends". This will automatically show users that their friends already like your page.

Facebook's approach to delivering video could not be more different. As a social media platform, Facebook is rarely used as a search engine. Most Facebook users are keeping up with friends and family in their newsfeed. For many users, Facebook is an immediate escape from boredom. The average user spends almost forty minutes a day looking for a mixture of friends, family, and entertainment. On Facebook, videos are generally delivered in between posts from a user's friend. This might sound awkward, but the platform is built for advertisers to succeed. There is a unique opportunity to delight Facebook users at the moment they are scrolling through a virtually endless newsfeed. Have you ever seen an advertisement on Facebook that mentioned other friends you have that like a sponsored post? Facebook can provide social proof for brands like no other platform.

While YouTube and Facebook are incredibly different, both offer endless advertising opportunities for businesses. YouTube's platforms leverage the innovative Google AdWords system. Many advertisers have been using this platform for years. Facebook has a similar online advertising platform. Unlike AdWords, Facebook has integrated advertising opportunities directly into the social media platform. Facebook will automatically recognize advertising opportunities and notify content owners below a post. For example, Facebook may tell you that your content is performing well with 35-55 year old males. Facebook will then suggest a targeted advertising campaign based on your regularly selected budget.

Many people don't realize that YouTube videos can be advertised with keywords. Unlike buying AdWord advertisements on the front page of Google, YouTube videos are either recommended or inserted into other videos on YouTube. AdWord clicks on Google's search engine can cost anywhere from one penny to hundreds of dollars each. These targeted keyword clicks are almost always more expensive than advertising videos. I have found the average cost per view on YouTube is generally $.01-.03. I do believe

FACEBOOK TIP

Facebook is a great place to learn about your audience. Facebook will tell you which demographics are responding best to your content.

that Google AdWord clicks are more valuable than YouTube video views in many ways. It's much easier to judge a user's intent to buy with keywords from a Google search versus a subscription to your YouTube channel. Most YouTube viewers are in the mood to watch the video. This is a great opportunity to prime viewers to interact further with your brand but it doesn't compare to a Google Search. On Google people are searching for something they want. No matter which platform you use, advertisers are only charged when a user actually clicks or watches a video. Advertisers are not usually charged for impressions.

Your Ad Has a High Relevance Score   ✕

Great work! Your ad has an average relevance score of 5, which means it's getting more positive feedback and is costing less to deliver than most ads on Facebook.

👥 2,542 people reached   Boost Post Again

The remarketing tools available from Google and Facebook take advertising values to another level. While demographic controls provide general guidance for audience building, remarketing to engaged users and website visitors offers advertisers higher probability of conversion.

Facebook's website viewer tracking tool is called the "Facebook Pixel." The Pixel is a piece of code that can be installed on your website to identify Facebook users that have visited your website for up to 180 days. Google has a similar tracking code. These codes help advertisers build up lists of people that are already familiar with your brand. You can trigger advertising campaigns to follow around users who have recently visited your website in a given amount of time. If a user visited in the past 24 hours perhaps you can create a special offer for them. Businesses small and large can target audiences based on very specific information. The amazing part about these platforms is that they become more powerful as you use them. Why advertise to the entire world when you have 100,000 people who have already visited your website without purchasing? Why wouldn't brands retarget their most engaged content consumers?

YouTube and Facebook offer unique audience building value. Unlike a webpage click, on YouTube and Facebook advertisers can grow audiences. Facebook calls their audiences "Likes" and YouTube simply calls these audiences "Subscribers." Once viewers like your Facebook page or subscribe to your YouTube channel, the platforms will start to deliver your content for free. YouTube subscribers are delivered digest emails about the latest content from the user's subscribers. The YouTube homepage will also prioritize content based on the user's subscriptions. Facebook will prioritize newsfeed information in a similar way.

Understanding the unique nuances on YouTube and Facebook is critical for successful social media marketing. New businesses using the platform need to learn how to effectively build an audience. For our business building, an audience of customers and prospects is the ultimate goal of social media marketing. Once your business has an audience, the likelihood of content being shared and organically ranking for searches greatly increases.

With audience building as a primary goal, businesses need to rethink their marketing goals. Creating content that turns strangers into subscribers becomes a top priority. The simplest tip to start with this goal is to simply ask viewers to like and subscribe to your channel inside every video. Give your viewers a list of compelling reasons why they should subscribe to your content. The next step is to study your analytics. Which videos are converting the most viewers into subscribers? Which videos are getting the most engagement? These are the videos you will want to continue advertising.

Our company's strategy is to advertise every video we make in order to generate viewer data. We use the viewer data to pick winners. A winning video either has a long view time average or a high average engagement from our audience. This process can cost as little as $5 per video. With a minimal budget, we can advertise to a healthy viewer sample size of 1,000 or more test subjects.

In general, Facebook offers a lot more detailed information about their users than Google. Facebook has gathered information about what people like, who they follow and who they are friends with. As an advertiser, we can use this information to deliver our videos to relevant audiences. Facebook also offers a lookalike tool which can take an email list of contacts and generate millions of related contacts based on five or more data points. Lookalike audiences are a gold mine for businesses looking for more customers based on a known set of ideal contacts.

I have found that YouTube and Google are ideal funnels for people who are already searching for your target keywords. On the flip side, Facebook is useful for helping people find you who aren't necessarily looking for you at all. Both platforms offer amazing audience building tools. They provide advertisers value above and beyond traditional media. In general, we have found that Facebook does a better job creating online communities. YouTube has added a "community" area to the platform, but its value is pale in comparison to Facebook. While Facebook wins for community building, YouTube wins for video shelf life. Since Facebook is not used as a search engine, the likelihood of someone finding your video after it has been advertised is very low. YouTube offers advertisers a much longer lifetime value for each video. In fact, YouTube videos are often displayed directly in Google search results. YouTube also provides superior value per view when it comes to terminology. Facebook considers three seconds a view, while YouTube considers thirty seconds a view.

In conclusion, I have found that using both platforms simultaneously will offer the fastest path to growth. There are unique audiences on each platform that should not be ignored. Mark Zuckerberg,

Facebook's CEO, has said that the platform will be 90% video by 2020. YouTube is essentially 100% video with premium TV offerings that now rival traditional cable TV packages. As these platforms optimize for video, live streaming becomes the holy grail for content creators. Facebook has released a report saying users watch live video on average three times longer than on-demand. Media consumers are prioritizing what they watch and the numbers prove content with live viewer engagement increase watch time. Currently, neither platform will allow for "live advertising." There have been rumors that Facebook is working on a way for creators to pay for advertising a live video. But until that happens, live video is a tool for content creators that kick-starts the social media algorithms. Once the video is available on-demand, all the same video advertising strategies apply. In early 2017, our company started to live stream our weekly broadcasts to both YouTube and Facebook at the same time. We engage both audiences and fuel our social media channels for incremental growth each week. Don't miss out on a year of live streaming! Take advantage of the early mover advantage and kick some butt out there!

Chapter 17: So How Do You Get Started?

So now let's talk about how to get started. I have interviewed quite a lot of people on the subject of live streaming and we have to address the fact that live video is *scary* for many people. It's much easier to say "cut," let's re-record that than to put yourself out there live for the world to see. One of the best ways to start training yourself or your team for streaming live video, is to start by recording short video clips live. Not only is this a great exercise that can produce amazing content for your company, but it will prime your talent for live production.

So, let's assume that your team is comfortable shooting quick videos from a single live take. If they mess up, they just record another session. At least we are starting to understand the value of making content in a live recording environment. Now it's time to start thinking about what we are going to need to be successful. Here are some of the key ingredients we have found to be extremely beneficial in the studio.

1. A dedicated host and co-host
2. A dedicated producer
3. A dedicated space
4. A regular show schedule
5. A regular show agenda

The first two are pretty obvious to me. Not everyone is going to be comfortable becoming your business's spokesperson. A good host or co-host is someone who can comfortably talk about almost anything and is willing to be your brand ambassador. Adding a co-host will make everyone's life easier and your audience is going to appreciate the extra layers of conversation. If you have a co-host, we have found that it can be effective to have one person assume the role of the audiences medium. Have one person regularly monitoring the chat room and asking questions on the audiences behalf. If your ultimate goal is to turn strangers into customers, having someone to connect with them during your live broadcast can work wonders. You can also show comments from your audience live on the screen. We usually have one of our hosts read the questions out loud. This provides social proof inside your videos when they watched live or on-demand.

If you have read along this far, you know that I started producing video content as the on-screen talent with my work laptop. If you are a one man band, I think that producing short video clips on camera is your best practice for preparing to go live. At a certain point we found that there is no real substitute for an in-studio producer. Many of the new live streaming shows include interview segments with their producer. This is an interesting way to add context to the live broadcast. We are doing this with our StreamGeeks show now, working Michael in as a third opinion and valued guest.

If your organization has someone who can assume the role of a producer, don't forget that your producer can likely become your photographer, your blogger, and even your social media distributor. Most live streaming shows are only once a week. So during the rest of the week you have an extra team member who knows the weeks agenda. They can be well prepared to assist with the digital media tasks at hand. Michael is a great photographer and often plans out amazing thumbnails for our videos before the show. After the show Michael is able to share the content with knowledge of the broadcast's content. As a team everyone is learning about our latest lesson at hand. We are furthering our internal education and simultaneously broadcasting to the world which is an amazing side benefit to the process.

Next you need to think about the vibe of your studio space. As you may remember, for me everything started in our companies conference room. I added a green screen and eventually carved out a little nook in the side of our shared meeting space. But things didn't really take shape until we moved into a new office and created a dedicated studio space. Everyone is different and finding your ideal space will likely take time. I was able to do quite a lot with a green screen. After that, the small nook in our conference room was the home for hundreds of online videos that increased in quality, one after the next. Choose a space that fits your personality.

STREAMING TIP

Always schedule your live broadcasts. On YouTube specifically it keeps all your views and watch time attributed to your video.

Scheduling your live show is almost as crucial as the content. Anyone who has a live show will tell you that sticking with a plan is the only way to succeed. I still remember our first live show when nobody showed up. But after five or ten episodes, all scheduled on Mondays at 11AM PST

/ 2PM EST, we started to attract an audience. People need to know when you're going live and after a while they will start to work you into their regular routine. If you use the "Live Now" feature on YouTube, you will not gain all the views and watch time on your on-demand video. Yes, you will need to enter in new RTMP stream keys every time this way, but it's totally worth it.

Finally, preparing a show agenda should become a regular routine. I would consider myself the executive producer of our show. As such I research and prepare all of the content each week. Usually, we have a detailed bullet point agenda with multiple built-in segments. The entire team will have access to the live Google Doc for collaboration and preparation before the show. Right before the show we will determine the best camera angles to use and roughly when we are going to switch focus. We do our best to keep everyone on the same page. The more preparation you do, the better your show will turn out.

Chapter 18: Monetizing Live Streaming with New Products & Services

For us, the video content we are creating monetizes itself. We are in a very unique situation where the process of improving our video production is just as important as the content we are covering. Many of our viewers will tune in just to see the latest technology we are using during our presentation. The conversation on our show often turns into a technical review outside the main presentation content. This is the perfect chance for our viewers to ask questions about our studio in an effort to increase their own show's production value. Just like a news channel, we want to make sure that there is always something fresh to talk about. But what about real businesses who want to add products and services to make more money in a growing world of live streaming?

We have interviewed over ten industry professionals who run businesses in the video production and live broadcasting space. Some have booming businesses serving the live streaming market and others are still just dipping their toes into the water. We have an hour long webinar on "how to add live streaming services to your business," which includes interviews with these business owners you may want to check out. But let's start with ten popular services businesses are adding to their portfolio.

- Service #1 - On-site Streaming / Setup / Training Programs
- Service #2 - Offering Studio Time
- Service #3 - Studio Build & Installation
- Service #4 - Show Design, Branding & Marketing
- Service #5 - Workflow Consulting - SEO Strategy
- Service #6 - Remote Management Camera Operation
- Service #7 - Custom Computer Builds
- Service #8 - Training for both Software and Hardware
- Service #9 - Post Production / Content Distribution
- Service #10 - Social Media Management

Live Streaming Services

Likely Buyer Journey / Customer Thought Process

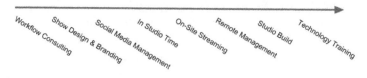

Workflow Consulting Show Design & Branding Social Media Management In Studio Time On-Site Streaming Remote Management Studio Build Technology Training

The most common service in the space today is on-site streaming and setup. Production groups are commonly being hired to live stream events for their customers. These customers either do not own the equipment necessary or do not have the skills required to live stream the event themselves. The opposite side of this business is selling time to customers who want to make content in a video production studio. This business model is very popular and has many benefits including the ability to create high quality video for yourself and your clients in the same space.

Setting up and installing permanent live streaming systems for customers is another booming market right now. The way these services are delivered vary quite a lot and the potential value add is quite high in many circumstances. One of my good friends, Tom Sinclair from Eastern Shore Broadcasting, just focuses on building and designing live streaming systems in his home office. Once assembled Tom ships the systems out to his customers and supports their DIY installation. He will design custom computers built to fit the needs of his customers. He also provides remote support and even sells most of the equipment required for the physical installation. This is a very cost effective business model. Most of Tom's customers are not located in his small town of Fairhope, Alabama as you could imagine.

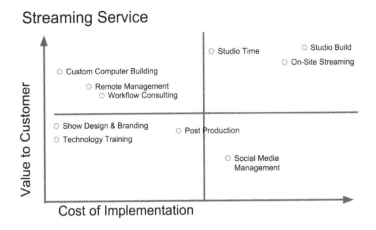

Streaming Service

Value to Customer (y-axis)
Cost of Implementation (x-axis)

- Studio Time
- Studio Build
- On-Site Streaming
- Custom Computer Building
- Remote Management
- Workflow Consulting
- Show Design & Branding
- Post Production
- Technology Training
- Social Media Management

Providing on-site installation for live streaming studios is perhaps the most valuable service on our list. It provides businesses the opportunity to make quite a lot of money and long lasting relationship with their clients. This business model is by no means new. The audio visual installation market here in the USA is a multi-billion dollar industry and there are massive companies that employ thousands who have been in business for 50+ years. While the market is large and competition abundant, there still lies a large opportunity for businesses that want to focus on live streaming specifically.

Another side of the live streaming market that can enhance many businesses is the marketing and consulting opportunities. During our interview series, available on our YouTube channel, we heard over and over again that the digital media landscape is very complicated for businesses to navigate. The thought of live streaming for many businesses is just another responsibility on top of social media posting, content creation, and the blogging they already don't have time for. Marketing and branding agencies are in a perfect position to help companies start a regular live streaming show. This way, they may be able to more effectively accomplish many of the goals they are already being hired for. Now that live streaming is so tightly knit with social media and end user engagement, the time is ripe for marketing companies to jump on board. It's just a matter of time until we see marketing companies add consulting packages focused on the live streaming industry.

Finally, post-production has always been a huge market in the video production world. Many of the business owners that we talked to who own video production companies are wary about offering live streaming services. But just like Krystal from Old Soul Decor, the video production and staging companies are starting to see the writing on the wall. Justin Chan, the owner of Valley Creek Productions, told us that they have only live streamed one event and the quality wasn't up to their standards. Bad experiences like this happen to the best of us before we know what we are doing. Traditional video production companies are in the perfect position to offer live event streaming services. Event and staging companies should be helping their customers live stream and charge for virtual attendance to their events.

Again, this is a problem we are trying to solve here at StreamGeeks by bringing together professionals from all over the industry in our interview series. We hope to provide perspective for businesses around the world. By showing the successful companies right next to the companies who had a bad first experience, we should be able to open everyone's eyes to the opportunities at hand. We interviewed marketing professionals, social media enthusiasts, on-site live streamers, video production companies, custom computer builders, and studio managers. This was an insightful StreamGeeks episode for anyone interested in adding live streaming services to their business.

Chapter 19: So What's Next?

So what's next for the StreamGeeks. We can't know for sure but I would like to paint a picture for you. Social media networks like Facebook and YouTube are going to grow more and more integrated into the fabric of society. They will slowly replace traditional television and deliver something truly new and innovative. Younger generations will wonder how we ever watched television without being able to click and select options.

Will everyone be wearing virtual reality headsets and taking self-driving cars to work? Yes, but not for a very long time. In the next couple of years, we are going see more and more video. Internet speeds will increase and access to high quality cellular networks will spread. The giant technology companies of the world will likely help pay for the infrastructure required to deliver their services. The last quarter of 2017 was the first time in United States history where the top five companies were all technology based. Yes, Amazon, Apple, Google, Facebook, and Microsoft are all going to have major roles to play in the future of video and technology. It's interesting to note that all of the top USA technology companies own major social media networks. Where will they take the industry?

Usually we can expect a technology adoption lifecycle that starts with the innovators and slowly moves into the early adoption stages. This is where we are now with live video. I firmly believe that the live streaming market is still in the early stages of technological adoption. Facebook Live just had it's first birthday and television is not completely dead yet. We have many years to come until we can say with certainty that the streaming media market has reached the early majority.

Over the Top Television or OTT media is a term that has been used to describe extraordinary content that is being delivered online. A great example of OTT would be a live show premier embedded onto a specialized website. In the future we will see purpose built online delivery systems made to enhance the viewing experience. We will see all kinds of innovation curating the way media is being delivered to end users. OTT content is going to be shocking and cool for everyone used to traditional television. But slowly this type of media delivery will become commonplace.

PAUL WILLIAM RICHARDS

Major growth in the live streaming industry will come from advertising opportunities. The live streaming protocol that we all use (RTMP) has always had additional layers of communication built into the protocol. The first two layers for audio and video are being used 24/7 every day. But the third layer which provides data can be used to embed links along with the streaming audio and video. For example, there is a layer inside the RTMP protocol that can be used to deliver viewers data such as a link to an ecommerce shop. Imagine if your favorite sports player just scored the game winning goal. Just then a link to buy the players jersey pops up on the screen. This is the type of advertising we will see in the next couple of years.

So, I truly believe our team has a lot to offer the live streaming industry. As you may have noticed … I love my job. Last week we outfit my Toyota 4Runner with live streaming cameras and took our viewers on a drive to Dunkin Donuts. That was the first time someone commented in the chat "I want your job." So, I would like to invite you to join our Facebook User Group. This group is a space where you can interact with others and check in on the inner workings of StreamGeeks.

The user group is also a great place to ask for suggestions. We regularly have individuals posting jobs for producers or on-screen talent. If you are looking to build a team just like I did, this is a great place to start! It's a community dedicated to helping each other and having fun.

Finally, there are a couple of parting resources I wanted to leave you with. First I want to give you the coupon codes to all of my video production courses. I have over 10,000 students taking these courses and I do my best to update the content with the latest available information in our industry. Download at https://ptzoptics.com/landing/coupons.html.

Second, we have a free PDF download called "The Ultimate Guide to Live Streaming" which features tips from seven of the industry top professionals. You can download this guide on the homepage of StreamGeeks. Live streaming is not a fad. It's a trend that is growing rapidly. Right now we are in the early adoption stages as of 2018. But I believe by 2020 we will be in the mass adoption stages of live streaming as social media and television start to merge. I look forward to seeing you in the chat!

Sincerely,

Paul Richards,

Chief Streaming Officer

StreamGeeks

paul.richards@streamgeeks.us

GLOSSARY OF TERMS

3.5mm Audio Cable - Male to male stereo cable, common in standard audio uses.

4K - A high definition resolution option (3840 x 2160 pixels or 4096 x 2160 pixels)

16:9 [16x9] - Aspect ratio of 9 units of height and 16 units of width. Used to describe standard HDTV, Full HD, non-HD digital television and analog widescreen television.

API [Application Program Interface]- A streaming API is a set of data a social media network uses to transmit on the web in real time. Going live directly from YouTube or Facebook uses their API.

Bandwidth - Bandwidth is measured in bits and the word "bandwidth" is used to describe the maximum data transfer rate.

Bitrate – Bitrates are used to select the data transfer size of your live stream. This is the number of bits per second that can be transmitted along a digital network.

Broadcasting - The distribution of audio or video content to a dispersed audience via any electronic mass communications medium.

Broadcast Frame Rates - Used to describe how many frames per second are captured in broadcasting. Common frame rates in broadcast include **29.97fps and 59.97 fps**.

Capture Card - A device with inputs and outputs that allow a camera to connect to a computer.

Chroma Key - A video effect that allows you to layer images and manipulate color hues [i.e. green screen] to make a subject transparent.

Cloud Based-Streaming - Streaming and video production interaction that occurs within the cloud, therefore accessible beyond a single user's computer device.

Color Matching - The process of managing color and lighting settings on multiple cameras to match their appearance.

Community Strategy - The strategy of building one's brand and product recognition by building meaningful relationships with an audience, partner, and clientele base.

Content Delivery Network [CDN] - A network of servers that deliver web-based content to an end user.

CPU [Central Processing Unit] – This is the main processor inside of your computer, and it is used to run the operating system and your live streaming software.

DAW - Digital Audio Workstation software is used to produce music. It can also be used to interface with multiple devices and other software using MIDI.

DB9 Cable - A common cable connection for camera joystick serial control.

DHCP [Dynamic Host Configuration Protocol] Router - A router with a network management protocol that dynamically sets IP addresses, so the server can communicate with its sources.

Encoder - A device or software that converts your video sources into an RTMP stream. The RTMP stream can be delivered to CDNs such as Facebook or YouTube.

FOH – Front of House is the part of your church that is open to the public. There is generally a FOH audio mix made to fill this space with the appropriate audio.

GPU – Graphics Processing Unit. This is your graphics card which is used for handling video inside your computer.

H.264 & H.265 - Common formats of video recording, compression, and delivery.

HDMI [High Definition Multimedia Interface] - A cable commonly used for transmitting audio/video.

HEVC [High Efficiency Video Coding] - H.265, is an advanced version of h.264 which promises higher efficiency but lacks the general support of h.264 among most software and hardware solutions available today.

IP [Internet Protocol] Camera/Video - A camera or video source that can send and receive information via a network & internet.

IP Control - The ability to control/connect a camera or device via a network or internet.

ISP – Internet Service Provider. This is the company that you pay monthly for your internet service. They will provide you with your internet connection and router.

Latency - The time it takes between sending a signal and the recipient receiving it.

Live Streaming - The process of sending and receiving audio and or video over the internet.

LAN [Local Area Network] - A network of computers linked together in one location.

MIDI [Musical Instrument Digital Interface] - A way to connect a sound or action to a device. (i.e. a keyboard or controller to trigger an action or sound on a stream

Multicast - Multicast is a method of sending data to multiple computers on your LAN without incurring additional bandwidth for each receiver. Multicast is very different from Unicast which is a data transport method that opens a unique stream of data between each sender and receiver. Multicast allows you to broadcast video from a single camera or live streaming computer to multiple destinations inside your church without adding the bandwidth burden on your network.

Multicorder – Also known as an "IsoCorder" is a feature of streaming software that allows the user to record raw footage from camera feed directly to your hard drive. This feature allows you to record multiple video sources at the same time.

NDI® [Network Device Interface] - Software standard developed by NewTek to enable video-compatible products to communicate, deliver, and receive broadcast quality video in high quality, low latency manner that is frame-accurate and suitable for switching in a live production environment.

NDI® Camera - A camera that allows you to send and receive video over your LAN using NDI technology.

NDI® | HX - NDI High Efficiency, optimizes NDI for limited bandwidth environments.

Network - A digital telecommunications network which allows nodes to share resources. In computer networks, computing devices exchange data with each other using connections between nodes.

Network Switch – A network switch is a networking device that connects multiple devices on a computer network using packet switching to receive, process and forward data to the destination device.

NTSC - Video standard used in North America.

OBS – Open Broadcaster Software is one of the industries most popular live streaming software solutions because it is completely free. OBS is available for Mac, PC, and Linux computers.

PAL - Analog video format commonly used outside of North America.

PCIe- Allows for high bandwidth communication between a device and the computer's motherboard. A PCIe card can installed inside a custom-built computer to provide multiple video inputs (such as HDMI or SDI).

PoE - Power over Ethernet.

PTZ - Pan, tilt, zoom.

RS-232 - Serial camera control transmission.

Router – Your internet router is generally provided to you by your internet service provider. This device may include a firewall, WiFi and/or network switch functionality. This device connects your network to the internet.

RTMP [Real Time Messaging Protocol] – Used for live streaming your video over the public internet.

RTSP [Real Time Streaming Protocol] - Network control protocol for streaming from one point to point. Generally, used for transporting video inside your local area network.

vMix® – vMix is a live streaming software built for Windows computers. It is a professional favorite with high-end features such as low latency capture, NDI support, instant replay, multi-view and much more.

Wirecast® – Wirecast is a live streaming software available for both Mac and PCs with advanced features such as five layers of overlays, lower thirds, virtual sets and much more.

xSplit® – xSplit is a live streaming software with a free and/or low monthly fee paid option. This is a great software available on for Windows computers that combines advanced features and simple to use interface.

About the Author

Paul is the Chief Streaming Officer for StreamGeeks. StreamGeeks is a group of video production experts dedicated to helping organizations discover the power of live streaming.

Every Monday, Paul and his team produce a live show in their downtown West Chester, Pennsylvania studio location. Having produced live shows as amateurs themselves, the StreamGeeks steadily worked their way to a professional level by learning from experience as they went.

Today, they have an impressive following and a tight-knit online community which they serve through consultations and live shows that continue to inspire, motivate, and inform organizations who refuse to settle for mediocrity. The show explores the ever-evolving broadcast and live streaming market while engaging a dedicated live audience.

As a husband and father raising his children in the Lutheran faith, Richards knows a thing or two about the technology inside the church. Richards now specializes in the live streaming media industry leveraging the technology for lead generation. In his book, "Live Streaming is Smart Marketing", Richards reveals his view on lead generation and social media.

Additional Online Courses:

Join over 20,000 other students learning how to leverage the power of live streaming! Take the following courses taught by Paul Richards for free by downloading the course coupon codes available at streamgeeks.us/start.

- **Facebook Live Streaming** - *Beginner*

This course will take your through the Facebook Live basics. It has already been updated twice! This also includes using Facebook Live Reactions!

- **YouTube Live Streaming** - *Beginner*

This course will take you through the YouTube Live basics. It also includes essential branding and tips for marketing.

- **Introduction to OBS (Open Broadcaster Software)**

This course will take your through one of the world's most popular FREE live streaming software solutions. OBS is a great place to start live streaming for free!

- **Introduction to xSplit Software** - *Beginner*

This course takes you through xSplit which has more features that OBS but costs roughly $5/month. Learn how to create amazing live productions and make videos much faster with xSplit!

- **Introduction to vMix** - *Intermediate*

vMix will have you live streaming like the Pros in no time. This Windows based software will amaze even the most advanced video producers!

- **Introduction to Wirecast** - *Intermediate*

Wirecast is the preferred software for so many professional live streamers. Available for Mac or PC this is the ideal software for anyone looking for professional streaming.

- **Introduction to NewTek NDI** - *Intermediate*

NewTek's innovative IP video standard NDI (Network Device Interface) will change the way you think about live video production. Learn how to use this innovative new technology for live streaming and video production system design.

- **Introduction to live streaming course** - *Beginner*

This course includes everything you need to get started designing your show. This course includes a starter pack of course files including: Photoshop, After Effects and free Virtual Sets.

- **Introduction to live streaming** - *Intermediate*

This course focuses on more advanced techniques for optimizing your production workflow and using compression to get the most out of your processor. This course includes files for: Photoshop, After Effects and free Virtual Sets.

- **Live Streaming for Good - Church Streaming Course** - *Intermediate*

This course focuses on live streaming for churches and houses of worship. We tackle some of the big questions about live streaming in a house of worship and dive into the specific challenges of this space.

- **How to Live Streaming A Wedding** - *Beginner*

This is a great course for anyone looking to start live streaming weddings. Originally designed for Wedding Photographers to add a live streaming service to their existing portfolio of offerings. This course is great for beginners

1